chicken

chicken

Sue Maggs

Photography by James Duncan

southwater

This edition is published by Southwater

Distributed in the UK by
The Manning Partnership
251–253 London Road East
Batheaston
Bath BA1 7RL
UK
tel. (0044) 01225 852 727
fax (0044) 01225 852 852

Distributed in the USA by
Ottenheimer Publishing
5 Park Center Court
Suite 300
Owing Mills MD 2117-5001
USA
tel. (001) 410 902 9100
fax (001) 410 902 7210

Distributed in Australia by
Sandstone Publishing
Unit 1, 360 Norton Street
Leichhardt
New South Wales 2040
Australia
tel. (0061) 2 9560 7888
fax (0061) 2 9560 7488

Distributed in New Zealand by
Five Mile Press NZ
PO Box 33-1071
Takapuna
Auckland 9
New Zealand
tel. (0064) 9 4444 144
fax (0064) 9 4444 518

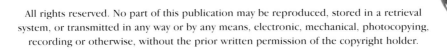

Southwater is an imprint of Anness Publishing Limited
© 1994, 2000 Anness Publishing Limited

1 3 5 7 9 10 8 6 4 2

Publisher: Joanna Lorenz
Series Editor: Lindsay Porter
Editor: Jane Royston
Designer: Peter Laws
Photographer: James Duncan
Stylist: Madeleine Brehaut
Assistant Home Economist: Lucy McKelvie

Previously published as *Step-by-step 50 Fantastic Chicken Dishes*

CONTENTS

INTRODUCTION

Chicken is popular with children and adults alike. It is versatile and economical, and can be cooked with a wide variety of ingredients and flavors. It is low in fat and quick to cook, with very little wastage.

Chicken can be bought in many forms; whole, quartered or jointed into thighs, drumsticks, breasts and wings, with or without bones and skin, which makes preparation very easy. Ground chicken can be found at some supermarkets, or, alternatively, the skinned flesh can be ground quickly in a food processor. Although it is convenient to buy portions individually packed, it is expensive. It is much cheaper to buy a whole chicken and prepare it yourself and cheaper still to buy a frozen chicken and defrost it thoroughly before using. The added bonus of a frozen chicken are the giblets (neck, heart, liver and gizzard) found inside the cavity of the chicken which can be used for making stock. To get the best results from a frozen bird, allow it to thaw slowly in the refrigerator until completely defrosted. Many types of chicken are available, and all are full of flavor. Some have added herbs and flavorings, and others are self-basting with either butter or olive oil injected into the flesh. This helps to keep the flesh succulent. Baby chickens are called poussins and can be bought to serve whole or halved depending on their size. In fact, chicken can be bought at any weight from 1 lb to 6 lb to suit the size of your family.

The recipes in this book are all based on a family of four people, but they can be easily halved for two or doubled for eight. There is a chapter on entertaining, and all of these recipes are for eight people, but you can adapt the quantities for four, or sixteen depending on your requirements.

Choosing a Chicken

When choosing a fresh chicken, it should have a plump breast and the skin should be creamy in color.

A bird's dressed weight is taken after plucking and drawing and may include the giblets (neck, gizzard, heart and liver). A frozen chicken must be thawed slowly and thoroughly in the refrigerator – never at room temperature. Rinse with cool water and pat dry with a paper towel. Always clean surfaces after preparing raw chicken and do not place cooked chicken where raw chicken has been.

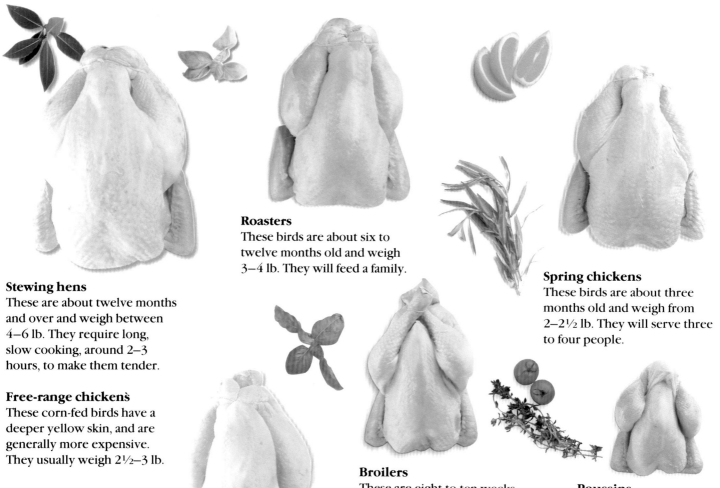

Roasters
These birds are about six to twelve months old and weigh 3–4 lb. They will feed a family.

Spring chickens
These birds are about three months old and weigh from 2–2½ lb. They will serve three to four people.

Stewing hens
These are about twelve months and over and weigh between 4–6 lb. They require long, slow cooking, around 2–3 hours, to make them tender.

Free-range chickens
These corn-fed birds have a deeper yellow skin, and are generally more expensive. They usually weigh 2½–3 lb.

Broilers
These are eight to ten weeks old and weigh 1½–2 lb. They will serve two people. Broilers are best roasted, broiled or pot-roasted.

Poussins
These are four to six weeks old and weigh 1–1¼ lb. Rock Cornish game hens can be substituted if desired.

Cuts of Chicken

Chicken pieces today are available pre-packaged in a variety of different ways. If you do not want to buy a whole bird, you can choose from the many selected cuts on the market. Most cooking methods are suitable for all cuts, but some are especially suited to specific cuts of meat.

Leg
This comprises the thigh and drumstick. Large pieces with bones, such as this, are suitable for slow-cooking, such as casseroling or poaching.

Skinless boneless thigh
This makes tasks such as stuffing and rolling much quicker, as it is already skinned and jointed.

Liver
This makes a wonderful addition to pâtés or to salads.

Drumstick
The drumstick is a firm favourite for barbecuing or frying, either in batter or rolled in breadcrumbs.

Wing
The wing does not supply much meat, and is often barbecued or fried.

Ground chicken
This is not as strongly flavoured as, say, ground beef, but may be used as a substitute in some recipes.

Breast
This comprises tender white meat and can be simply cooked in butter, as well as stuffed.

Thigh
The thigh is suitable for casseroling and other slow-cooking methods.

Jointing a Chicken

For recipes that call for chicken joints, it is often cheaper to buy a whole chicken and joint it yourself, particularly if you are cooking for a large number of people. It is important to have a portion of bone with the wing and breast joints, otherwise the flesh shrinks during cooking.

1 Hold the chicken firmly with one hand. Using a sharp knife, cut the skin between the leg and breast.

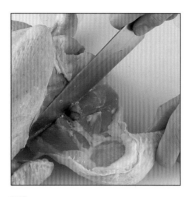

2 Then press the leg down to expose the ball-and-socket joint, cut or break the joint apart, and cut down towards the parson's nose.

3 Turn the chicken over and loosen the 'oyster' from the underside (lying embedded alongside the backbone). Repeat with the other leg.

4 Now with your finger, feel for the end of the breastbone, and with a sharp knife, cut diagonally through the flesh to the rib cage. (This will give each wing joint a good portion of breast meat.)

5 With strong kitchen scissors, cut through the rib cage and wishbone, separating the two wing joints.

6 Twist the wing tip (pinion) and tuck it under the breast meat so that the joint is held flat. This will give it a good shape for cooking.

7 With strong kitchen scissors, cut the breast meat from the carcass in one piece. (All that remains from the carcass is half of the rib cage and the backbone with the parson's nose attached.)

8 The legs can be cut in half through the joint to give a thigh joint and a drumstick. The breast can also be cut into two pieces through the breastbone.

Boning a Chicken

For the purpose of stuffing and to make carving simple, it is essential to bone a chicken. Use a sharp knife with a short blade. Work in short, scraping movements, keeping the knife against the bone at all times, to leave the carcass clean.

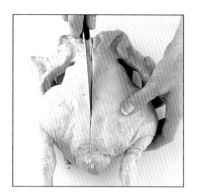

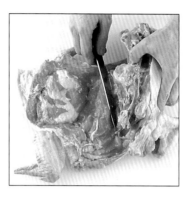

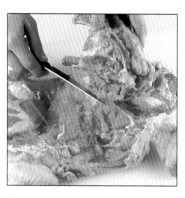

1 Remove any trussing string. Cut off the wing tips (pinions) and discard. With a short bladed, sharp knife cut the skin along the underside (backbone) of the chicken. Work the skin and flesh away from the carcass with the knife until the leg joints are exposed.

2 Cut the sinew between the ball-and-socket joints. This joins the thigh bones and wings to the carcass.

3 Holding the rib cage away from the chicken body, carefully scrape the breastbone clean and cut the carcass away from the skin. Take great care not to cut through the skin, or the stuffing will burst out of the hole.

4 Take hold of the thigh bone in one hand, and with the knife scrape the flesh down the bone to the next joint.

5 Cut around the joint and continue cleaning the drumstick until the whole leg bone is free. Repeat with the other leg and both the wings. Lay the chicken flat and turn the flesh of the legs and wings inside the chicken. Flatten the flesh neatly ready for stuffing.

Trussing a Chicken

Trussing a chicken means tying it into a good shape for cooking and carving. An untrussed chicken will collapse and the legs will splay open during cooking. It will also look very untidy when brought to the table for serving.

1 Fold the flap of neck skin under the chicken (encasing any stuffing) and tuck the wing tips (pinions) backwards and under the chicken, to hold the skin in place. Turn the bird on its back, press the legs down and into its sides to plump up the breast and give it a good shape. Thread a trussing needle (a needle about 10 in long) with a piece of fine string, long enough to thread through the bird and back again.

2 Insert the trussing needle through the wing joint, between the two small bones, and then through the body to emerge in the same position on the other side.

3 Re-insert the needle into the other end of the wing joint (making a long stitch) and pass the needle back through the body and out at the corresponding position of the opposite wing joint.

4 Tie the two pieces of string together forming another long stitch.

5 Re-thread the trussing needle and insert through the drumstick next to the joint on the leg, and through the body cavity to the opposite leg.

6 Insert back through the lower end of the drumsticks and tie the two thread ends firmly together.

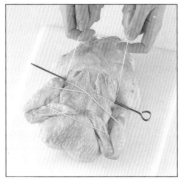

7 Alternatively, you can use a skewer and a piece of string. Push the skewer through the chicken below the thigh bone, turn it on to its breast and loop string around the wings, crossing it over to hold them firmly in place. Pass the string under the ends of the skewer and criss-cross over the back of the chicken.

8 Turn the bird over and bring the string up to tie the drumsticks and parson's nose together.

Stuffing a Chicken

Stuffing helps to keep chickens moist during cooking because they have very little fat. The stuffing also helps to make the meal go further. There are many different flavors that may be used to enhance the taste of chicken, without detracting from its own delicate flavor. Bread, rice, and potatoes can be used as the basis to which other ingredients may be added. Fat is important in stuffing because it prevents it from becoming dry and crumbly.

1 Only stuff the small neck-end of the chicken and not the large cavity inside the carcass, as the heat from the oven will not penetrate all the way through the chicken. Any left-over stuffing should be made into small balls and fried separately or put into a shallow, buttered ovenproof dish and baked in the oven with the chicken and cut into squares for serving.

2 Never pack the stuffing too tightly, as breadcrumbs will expand during cooking and this may cause the skin to burst open.

3 The flap of neck skin should then be tucked under the chicken and secured with the wing tips (pinions) or sewn into place with a needle and fine string. Remember to weigh the chicken after it has been stuffed to calculate the cooking time accurately.

Spatchcocking

This is a good way to broil or barbecue small chickens. By removing the backbones, the chickens can be opened out and flattened ready for cooking. Skewers are threaded through to maintain the shape.

1 Using a very sharp pair of kitchen scissors, cut the chicken on either side of its backbone.

2 Flatten the bird with the palm of your hand or a rolling pin. Turn it over and cut away the fine rib cage, leaving the rest of the carcass intact to hold its shape.

3 Thread thin skewers through the legs and wings to hold them in position and keep the bird flat. Brush liberally with melted butter, as a small chicken contains no fat to protect it during cooking. It will take about 10–15 minutes on each side depending on the heat.

Roasting a Chicken

Chickens have very little fat and the flesh can become dry if not protected during roasting. Lean bacon rashers or well-buttered tin foil can be used or, better still, both. Roasting bags are available and if the instructions are followed, work extremely well. The chicken browns nicely and stays moist during cooking.

COOKING TIMES
Allow 20 minutes per 1 lb plus 20 minutes added to the total cooking time. Remember to weigh the chicken *after* stuffing, to calculate the times.

ROASTING TIMES
Poussin
1–1¼ lb
roast for 40–45 minutes

Broiler
1½–2 lb
roast for 55–60 minutes

Spring chicken
2–2½ lb
roast for 1–1¼ hours

Roaster
3–4 lb
roast for 1 hour 20 minutes–1 hour 40 minutes

Stewing hen
4–6 lb
roast for 2–3 hours

1 Preheat the oven to 375°F. Remove all packaging from the cavity of the bird. Wash the chicken and pat dry. Season the inside of the chicken with salt and freshly ground black pepper and stuff if required. Truss the chicken and spread the breast with butter or lard.

2 Set the bird breast up on a rack in a roasting pan and season all over.

3 Roast the bird, basting it every 10 minutes after the first 30 minutes with the juices in the pan. If the chicken is browning too quickly it may be covered loosely with foil.

THAWING A FROZEN CHICKEN
Allow it to defrost slowly on a plate in the refrigerator for 36 hours. This slow thawing seems to make the chicken more tender. If you are in a hurry, however, defrost under cold running water. Never defrost a chicken at room temperature as this can breed salmonella. It is important that all the water crystals have melted and that the flesh is soft and pliable before it is cooked.

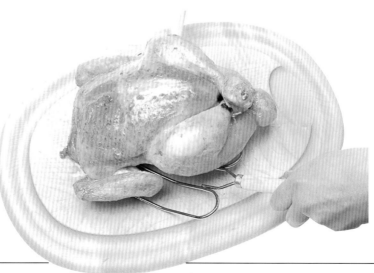

4 Transfer the chicken to a carving board and leave to rest for at least 15 minutes before serving. Make a simple gravy as instructed on the next page.

Carving a Chicken

It is best to allow the chicken to stand for 10–15 minutes before carving (while the gravy is being made). This allows the meat to relax and the flesh will not tear while carving. Use a sharp carving knife and work on a plate that will catch any juices that can be added to the gravy. The leg can be cut into two for a thigh and a drumstick.

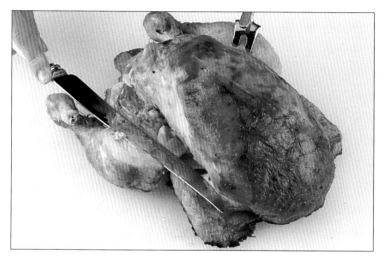

1 Hold the chicken firmly with a carving fork, between the breast and leg, down to the backbone. Cut the skin around the opposite leg and press gently outwards to expose the ball-and-socket joint. Cut through this and slip the knife under the back to remove the 'oyster' with the leg.

2 With the knife at the top end of the breastbone, cut down parallel on one side of the wishbone to take a good slice of breast meat with the wing joint.

3 With the knife at the end of the breastbone, cut down the front of the carcass, removing the wishbone. Carve the remaining breast into slices.

How to Make Gravy

Transfer the chicken to a serving dish. Remove any trussing string, cover loosely with the foil and stand in a warm place to allow the flesh to relax before carving. Spoon the fat from the juices in the roasting pan. Stirring constantly, blend 1 tbsp flour into the juices and cook gently until golden brown. Add 1¼ cups of chicken stock or vegetable cooking water and bring to a boil, to thicken. Season to taste with salt and pepper. Strain into a pitcher or gravy boat to serve.

Poaching

Poaching is a gentle cooking method, and produces stock for making a sauce afterwards.

1 Put the chicken into a flameproof casserole with bouquet garni (bay leaf, thyme and parsley), carrot and onion.

2 Cover with water and add salt and peppercorns. Bring to a boil, cover and simmer for about 1½ hours or until tender.

3 Cool in the liquid or lift out, shred, and add to a white sauce.

Casseroling

This slow-cooking method is good for large chicken joints with bones, or more mature meat.

1 Heat olive oil in a flameproof casserole and brown the chicken joints.

2 Add stock, wine or a mixture of both to a depth of 1 in. Add seasonings and herbs, cover, and cook on the stove or in the oven for 1¼ hours or until tender.

3 Add a selection of lightly fried vegetables such as pearl onions, mushrooms, carrots and small new potatoes about half-way through the cooking time.

Braising

This method can be used for whole chickens and pieces and is ideal for strongly flavored meat.

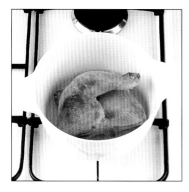

1 Heat olive oil in a flameproof casserole and lightly fry a whole bird or chicken joints until golden.

2 Remove the chicken and fry 1 lb of diced vegetables such as carrots, onions, celery and turnips until soft.

3 Replace the chicken, cover with a tight lid, and cook very slowly on the stove or in the oven preheated to 325°F until tender.

Chicken Stock

This all-purpose chicken stock may be used as the basis for a wonderful homemade soup.

1 Put the giblets (the neck, gizzard and heart, but not the liver, as this makes stock bitter), or the carcass from a cooked chicken, into a pan and just cover with water.

2 Add a quartered onion, carrot, bouquet garni (bay leaf, thyme and parsley) and a few peppercorns. Bring to a boil, cover and simmer gently for 1–2 hours.

3 Remove any scum that rises to the surface with a slotted draining spoon. Alternatively, make the stock when you cook the chicken, by putting the giblets in the roasting pan around the chicken with the onion and herbs and just enough water to stop them from burning. Add a little salt during cooking but not too much or the stock will become too salty as the liquid reduces down during cooking.

4 When the stock has set, remove the fat from the surface with a spoon.

Frying

Ensure that the chicken pieces are dry before frying, as any moisture will cause spitting.

1 To pan-fry chicken, heat oil or a mixture of oil and butter in a heavy-based frying pan over medium heat. When the fat is very hot, put in the chicken pieces, skin side down. Cook in batches if necessary to ensure even cooking.

2 Turn the pieces so they cook evenly, and fry until thoroughly cooked and deep golden brown all over. Dark meat will take longer to cook than white meat. Remove the pieces as they are cooked, and drain on paper towels.

3 To deep-fry chicken, dip the pieces in beaten egg, or a mixture of beaten egg and milk, then coat in seasoned flour or batter. If using seasoned flour, allow to set for 20 minutes before frying.

4 Half-fill a deep pan with vegetable oil and heat it to 365°F. To check the temperature, drop a cube of bread into the hot oil. If it takes 30 seconds to brown, the oil is hot enough.

5 Using a spatula or tongs, lower the chicken pieces into the oil, a few at a time. Turn to color evenly, and deep-fry until golden brown and cooked through.

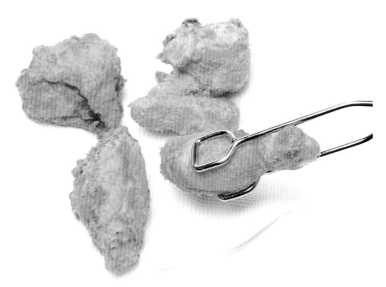

6 Remove from the oil and drain on paper towels. To keep hot while you fry the remaining pieces, place uncovered in the oven at a low temperature.

Bread Sauce

Bread sauce is one of the classic accompaniments to a traditional roast chicken.

Serves 4–6

INGREDIENTS
1 medium onion, peeled
4 whole cloves
1 bay leaf
2½ cups milk
2 cups fresh white bread crumbs
2 tbsp butter
salt and freshly ground black pepper

1 Peel the onion and then stick the cloves into it.

2 Put the onion, bay leaf and milk into a large pan and bring to a boil. Remove from the heat, cover and leave to infuse for 15 minutes.

3 Strain the liquid and add the bread crumbs and the butter.

4 Cook uncovered, over a very low heat for 10–15 minutes or until thickened, stirring constantly. Season with salt and freshly ground black pepper to taste. Cover with buttered waxed paper until needed to prevent a skin forming.

Chicken Liver Pâté

This low fat pâté is excellent served as a first course or a snack spread on melba toast or savory biscuits.

Serves 6

INGREDIENTS
1 tbsp olive oil
1 medium onion, chopped
1 garlic clove, crushed
1 lb trimmed chicken livers
2 tbsp brandy or sherry
1 tbsp chopped fresh parsley
1 tsp dried mixed herbs
scant cup low fat cream cheese or
   ricotta
salt and freshly ground black pepper

1 Heat the oil and cook the onion and garlic until tender. Add the livers.

2 Fry the livers until brown and crisp around the edges, about 5 minutes, or until no longer pink. Add the brandy or sherry, seasoning and herbs. Liquidize in a blender or food processor until smooth and leave to cool completely.

3 Stir in the cream cheese or ricotta. Serve in small dishes.

COOK'S TIP
The pâté will last for two to three days if kept covered in the refrigerator.

Basic Herb Stuffing

INGREDIENTS
1 small onion, finely chopped
1 tbsp butter
2 cups fresh bread crumbs
1 tbsp chopped fresh parsley
1 tsp dried mixed herbs
1 egg, beaten
salt and freshly ground black pepper

1 Cook the onion gently in the butter until tender. Allow to cool.

2 Add to the remaining ingredients and then mix thoroughly. Season well with salt and pepper.

VARIATIONS

Any of these ingredients may be added to the basic recipe in order to vary the flavor of the stuffing, depending on what you have in your kitchen cupboard.

1 stalk celery, finely chopped
1 small apple, diced
$\frac{1}{2}$ cup chopped walnuts or almonds
1 tbsp raisins or sultanas
$\frac{1}{4}$ cup chopped ready-to-eat dried prunes or apricots
$\frac{1}{2}$ cup finely chopped mushrooms
grated rind of $\frac{1}{2}$ orange or lemon
$\frac{1}{2}$ cup pine nuts
2 oz chopped lean bacon

Apricot and Orange Stuffing

INGREDIENTS
1 small onion, finely chopped
1 tbsp butter
2 cups fresh bread crumbs
$\frac{1}{4}$ cup finely chopped ready-to-eat dried apricots
grated rind of $\frac{1}{2}$ orange
1 small egg, beaten
1 tbsp chopped fresh parsley
salt and freshly ground black pepper

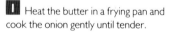

1 Heat the butter in a frying pan and cook the onion gently until tender.

2 Allow to cool slightly, and add to the rest of the ingredients.

3 Mix until thoroughly combined and season with salt and pepper.

Parsley, Lemon and Thyme Stuffing

INGREDIENTS
2 cups fresh bread crumbs
2 tbsp butter
1 tbsp chopped fresh parsley
½ tsp dried thyme
grated rind of ¼ lemon
1 rasher lean bacon, chopped
1 small egg, beaten
salt and freshly ground black pepper

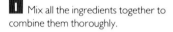 Mix all the ingredients together to combine them thoroughly.

Raisin and Nut Stuffing

INGREDIENTS
2 cups fresh bread crumbs
⅓ cup raisins
½ cup walnuts, almonds, pistachios
    or pine nuts
1 tbsp chopped fresh parsley
1 tsp chopped mixed herbs
1 small egg, beaten
2 tbsp melted butter
salt and freshly ground black pepper

1 Mix all the ingredients together thoroughly, and then season well with salt and pepper.

Sausage Stuffing

INGREDIENTS
1 tbsp butter
1 small onion, finely chopped
2 rashers lean bacon, chopped
8 oz ground sausage
½ tsp mixed dried herbs
salt and freshly ground black pepper

1 Heat the butter in a frying pan and cook the onion until tender. Add the bacon and cook for 5 more minutes, then allow to cool.

2 Add to the remaining ingredients and mix thoroughly.

Chicken Roulades

These chicken rolls make a light lunch dish for two, or a starter for four. They can be sliced and served cold with a salad.

Makes 4

INGREDIENTS
4 boned and skinned chicken thighs
4 oz chopped frozen spinach
1 tbsp butter
2 tbsp pine nuts
pinch of ground nutmeg
7 tbsp fresh white bread crumbs
4 rashers lean bacon
2 tbsp olive oil
²⁄₃ cup white wine or fresh or canned chicken stock
2 tsp cornstarch
2 tbsp light cream
1 tbsp chopped fresh chives
salt and freshly ground black pepper

bread crumbs
bacon
spinach
butter
pine nuts
chives
olive oil
light cream
chicken thighs
cornstarch

1 Preheat the oven to 350°F. Place the chicken thighs between two sheets of plastic wrap and flatten with a rolling pin.

2 Put the spinach and butter into a saucepan, heat gently until the spinach has defrosted, then increase the heat and cook rapidly, stirring occasionally until all the moisture has evaporated. Add the pine nuts, seasoning, nutmeg and fresh bread crumbs.

3 Divide the filling between the chicken pieces and roll up neatly. Wrap a rasher of bacon around each piece and secure with string.

4 Heat the oil in a large frying pan and brown the rolls all over. Drain through a slotted spoon and place in a shallow ovenproof dish.

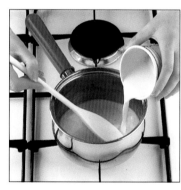

5 Pour over the wine or stock, cover, and bake for 15–20 minutes, or until tender. Transfer the chicken to a serving plate and remove the string. Strain the cooking liquid into a saucepan.

6 Mix the cornstarch to a smooth paste with a little cold water and add to the juices in the pan, along with the cream. Bring to a boil to thicken, stirring all the time. Adjust the seasoning and add the chives. Pour the sauce round the chicken and serve.

Chicken Soup

A thick, chunky chicken and vegetable soup served with garlic-flavored fried croûtons. A meal in itself.

Serves 4

INGREDIENTS
4 boned and skinned chicken thighs
1 tbsp butter
2 small leeks, thinly sliced
2 tbsp long grain rice
3¾ cups fresh or canned chicken
    stock
1 tbsp chopped mixed fresh parsley
    and mint
salt and freshly ground black pepper

FOR THE GARLIC CROÛTONS
2 tbsp olive oil
1 garlic clove, crushed
4 slices of bread, cut into cubes

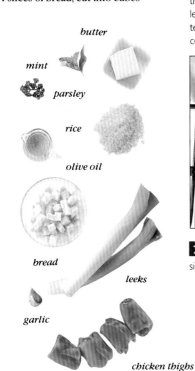

butter

mint

parsley

rice

olive oil

bread

leeks

garlic

chicken thighs

1 Cut the chicken into ½ in cubes. Melt the butter in a saucepan, then add the leeks and cook them until they are tender. Add the rice and chicken and cook for a further 2 minutes.

2 Add the stock, then cover and simmer for 15–20 minutes until tender.

3 To make the garlic croûtons, heat the oil in a large frying pan. Add the crushed garlic clove and bread cubes and cook until golden brown, stirring all the time to prevent burning. Drain on paper towels and sprinkle with a pinch of salt.

4 Add the parsley and mint to the soup and adjust the seasoning. Serve with garlic croûtons passed round separately.

Chicken Cigars

These small crispy rolls can be served warm as canapés with a drink before a meal, or as a first course with a crisp, colorful salad.

Serves 4

INGREDIENTS
1 × 10 oz package of filo pastry
3 tbsp olive oil
fresh parsley, to garnish

FOR THE FILLING
12 oz ground raw chicken
salt and freshly ground black pepper
1 egg, beaten
½ tsp ground cinnamon
½ tsp ground ginger
2 tbsp raisins
1 tbsp olive oil
1 small onion, finely chopped

raisins
olive oil
cinnamon
ground chicken
ginger
onion
egg
parsley
filo pastry

1 Mix all the filling ingredients, except the oil and onion, together in a bowl. Heat the oil in a large frying pan and cook the onion until tender. Leave to cool, then add the remaining mixed ingredients.

2 Preheat the oven to 350°F. Once the filo pastry package has been opened, keep the pastry completely covered at all times with a damp dish towel. Work fast, as the pastry dries out very quickly when exposed to the air. Unravel the pastry and cut into even 10 × 4 in strips.

3 Take one strip of pastry, cover the remainder, brush with a little oil and place a small spoonful of the filling about ½ in from the end.

4 To encase the filling, fold the sides inwards to a width of 2 in and roll into a cigar shape. Place on a greased baking sheet and brush with oil. Bake for about 20–25 minutes until golden brown and crisp. Garnish with fresh parsley.

Chicken Goujons

Serve as a first course for eight people or as a filling main course for four. Delicious served with new potatoes and salad.

Serves 8

INGREDIENTS
4 boned and skinned chicken breasts
3 cups fresh bread crumbs
1 tsp ground coriander
2 tsp ground paprika
½ tsp ground cumin
3 tbsp all-purpose flour
2 eggs, beaten
oil, for deep-frying
salt and freshly ground black pepper
lemon slices, to garnish
sprigs of fresh coriander, to garnish

FOR THE DIP
1¼ cups plain yogurt
2 tbsp lemon juice
4 tbsp chopped fresh coriander
4 tbsp chopped fresh parsley

bread crumbs
flour
eggs
lemon
yogurt
coriander
parsley
chicken breast

1 Divide the chicken breasts into two natural fillets. Place them between two sheets of plastic wrap and, using a rolling pin, flatten each one to a thickness of about ¼ in.

2 Cut into 1 in strips diagonally across the fillets.

3 Mix the bread crumbs with the spices and seasoning. Toss the chicken fillet pieces (goujons) into the flour, keeping them separate.

4 Dip the fillets into the beaten egg and then coat in the bread crumb mixture.

5 Thoroughly mix all the ingredients for the dip together, and season to taste. Chill until required.

6 Heat the oil in a heavy-based pan. It is ready for deep-frying when a cube of bread tossed into the oil sizzles on the surface. Fry the goujons in batches until golden and crisp. Drain on paper towels and keep warm in the oven until all the chicken has been fried. Garnish with lemon slices and sprigs of fresh coriander.

Spiced Chicken Livers

Chicken livers can be bought frozen, but make sure that you defrost them thoroughly before using. Serve as a first course or light meal along with a mixed salad and garlic bread.

Serves 4

INGREDIENTS
12 oz chicken livers
1 cup all-purpose flour
½ tsp ground coriander
½ tsp ground cumin
½ tsp ground cardamom seeds
¼ tsp ground paprika
¼ tsp ground nutmeg
6 tbsp olive oil
salt and freshly ground black pepper
garlic bread, to serve

chicken livers

olive oil

flour

coriander

cardamom seeds

cumin

paprika

nutmeg

1 Dry the chicken livers on paper towels, removing any unwanted pieces. Cut the large livers in half and leave the smaller ones whole.

2 Mix the flour with all the spices and the seasoning.

3 Coat the first batch of livers with spiced flour, separating each piece. Heat the oil in a large frying pan and fry the livers in small batches. (This helps to keep the oil temperature high and prevents the flour from becoming soggy.)

4 Fry quickly, stirring frequently, until crispy. Keep warm and repeat with the remaining livers. Serve immediately with warm garlic bread.

Nutty Chicken Balls

Serve these as a first course with the lemon sauce, or make into smaller balls and serve on wooden sticks as canapés.

Serves 4

INGREDIENTS
12 oz boneless chicken
½ cup unsalted pistachio nuts, finely
  chopped
1 tbsp lemon juice
2 eggs, beaten
all-purpose flour, for shaping
½ cup blanched chopped almonds
¾ cup dried bread crumbs
salt and freshly ground black pepper

FOR THE LEMON SAUCE
⅔ cup fresh or canned chicken stock
1¼ cups low fat cream cheese
1 tbsp lemon juice
1 tbsp chopped fresh parsley
1 tbsp snipped fresh chives

1 Skin and grind or chop the chicken finely. Mix with salt and freshly ground black pepper, pistachio nuts, lemon juice, and one beaten egg.

chopped almonds

minced chicken

chives

pistachio nuts

lemon

bread crumbs

parsley

cream cheese

2 Shape into sixteen small balls with floured hands (use a spoon as a guide, so that all the balls are roughly the same size). Roll the balls in the remaining beaten egg and coat with the almonds first and then the dried bread crumbs, pressing on firmly. Chill until ready to cook.

3 Preheat the oven to 375°F. Place at regular intervals on a greased baking sheet and bake for about 15 minutes or until golden brown and crisp.

4 To make the lemon sauce, gently heat the chicken stock and cream cheese together in a pan, whisking until smooth. Add the lemon juice, herbs and season to taste. Serve with the chicken balls.

French Chicken Salad

A light first course for eight people or a substantial main course for four. Arrange attractively on individual plates to serve.

Serves 8

INGREDIENTS
1 × 3½ lb free-range chicken
1¼ cups white wine and water, mixed
24 × ¼ in slices French bread
1 garlic clove, peeled
8 oz green beans
4 oz fresh young spinach leaves
2 stalks celery, thinly sliced
2 scallions, thinly sliced
2 sun-dried tomatoes, chopped
fresh chives and parsley, to garnish

FOR THE VINAIGRETTE
2 tbsp red wine vinegar
6 tbsp olive oil
1 tbsp whole grain mustard
1 tbsp honey
2 tbsp chopped mixed fresh herbs, e.g. thyme, parsley and chives
2 tsp finely chopped capers
salt and freshly ground black pepper

honey   *olive oil*

free-range chicken

red wine vinegar

spinach   *green beans*

1 Preheat the oven to 375°F. Put the chicken into a casserole with the wine and water. Roast for 1½ hours until tender. Leave to cool in the liquid. Remove the skin and bones and cut the flesh into small pieces.

2 To make the vinaigrette, put all the ingredients into a screw-topped jar and shake vigorously to emulsify. Adjust the seasoning to taste.

3 Toast the French bread under the broiler or in the oven until dry and golden brown, then lightly rub with the peeled garlic clove.

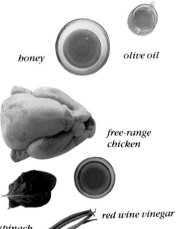

4 Trim the green beans, cut into 2 in lengths and cook in boiling water until just tender (*al dente*). Drain and rinse under cold running water.

5 Wash the spinach thoroughly, remove the stalks and tear into small pieces. Arrange on serving plates with the sliced celery, green beans, scallions, chicken and sun-dried tomatoes.

6 Spoon over the vinaigrette dressing. Arrange the toasted croûtons on top, garnish with extra fresh chives and parsley, if desired, and serve immediately.

Tagine of Chicken

Based on a traditional Moroccan dish. The chicken and couscous can be cooked the day before and reheated for serving.

Serves 8

INGREDIENTS
8 chicken legs (thighs and
    drumsticks)
2 tbsp olive oil
1 medium onion, finely chopped
2 garlic cloves, crushed
1 tsp ground turmeric
½ tsp ground ginger
½ tsp ground cinnamon
scant 2 cups fresh or canned chicken
    stock
1¼ cups pitted green olives
1 lemon, sliced
salt and freshly ground black pepper
fresh coriander sprigs, to garnish

FOR THE VEGETABLE COUSCOUS
2½ cups fresh or canned chicken
    stock
1 lb couscous
4 zucchini, thickly sliced
2 carrots, thickly sliced
2 small turnips, peeled and cubed
3 tbsp olive oil
1 × 15 oz can chick peas, drained

onion, green olives, ginger, cinnamon, turmeric, couscous, lemon, turnip, garlic, coriander, carrot, chick peas, zucchini, chicken stock, olive oil, chicken

1 Preheat the oven to 350°F. Cut the chicken legs into two through the joint.

2 Heat the oil in a large flameproof casserole and working in batches, brown the chicken on both sides. Remove and keep warm.

3 Add the onion and crushed garlic to the flameproof casserole and cook gently until tender. Add the spices and cook for 1 minute. Pour over the stock, bring to a boil, and return the chicken. Cover and bake for 45 minutes until tender.

4 Transfer the chicken to a bowl, cover and keep warm. Remove any fat from the cooking liquid and boil to reduce by one-third. Meanwhile, blanch the olives and lemon slices in a pan of boiling water for 2 minutes until the lemon skin is tender. Drain and add to the cooking liquid, adjusting the seasoning to taste.

5 To cook the couscous, bring the stock to a boil in a large pan and sprinkle in the couscous slowly, stirring all the time. Remove from the heat, cover and leave to stand for 5 minutes.

COOK'S TIP

The couscous can be reheated with 2 tbsp olive oil in a steamer over a pan of boiling water, stirring occasionally. If you cook the chicken in advance, undercook it by 15 minutes and reheat in the oven for 20–30 minutes.

6 Meanwhile, cook the vegetables, drain and put them into a large bowl. Add the couscous and oil and season. Stir the grains to fluff them up, add the chick peas and finally the chopped coriander. Spoon onto a large serving plate, cover with the chicken pieces, and spoon over the liquid. Garnish with fresh coriander sprigs.

Spanish Chicken

A colorful one pot dish, ideal for entertaining and delicious served with a crisp mixed green salad.

Serves 8

INGREDIENTS
2 tbsp all-purpose flour
2 tsp ground paprika
½ tsp salt
16 chicken drumsticks
4 tbsp olive oil
5 cups fresh or canned chicken stock
1 onion, finely chopped
2 garlic cloves, crushed
1 lb long grain rice
2 bay leaves
2 cups diced cooked ham
1 cup pimento-stuffed green olives
1 green pepper, seeded and diced
2 × 14 oz cans chopped tomatoes, with their juice
fresh parsley, to garnish

bay leaves

ham

long grain rice

paprika

pepper

chicken

onion

parsley

tomatoes

flour

1 Preheat the oven to 350°F. Shake together the flour, paprika and salt in a plastic bag, then add the drumsticks and toss to coat thoroughly.

2 Heat the oil in a large flameproof casserole and, working in batches, brown the chicken slowly on both sides. Remove and keep warm.

3 Meanwhile, bring the stock to a boil and add the onion, crushed garlic, rice and bay leaves. Cook for 10 minutes. Draw aside and add the ham, olives, peppers, and canned tomatoes with their juice.

4 Arrange the chicken on top, cover and bake for 30–40 minutes or until tender. Add a little more stock if necessary to prevent it from drying out. Remove the bay leaves and garnish with fresh parsley.

Chicken and Fruit Salad

The chickens may be cooked a day before eating and the salad finished off on the day of the party. Serve with warm garlic bread.

Serves 8

INGREDIENTS
4 tarragon or rosemary sprigs
2 × 3½ lb chickens
5 tbsp softened butter
⅔ cup fresh or canned chicken stock
⅔ cup white wine
1 cup walnut pieces
1 small cantaloupe
lettuce leaves
1 lb seedless grapes or pitted cherries
salt and freshly ground black pepper

FOR THE DRESSING
2 tbsp tarragon vinegar
8 tbsp light olive oil
2 tbsp chopped mixed fresh herbs,
  e.g. parsley, mint and tarragon

lettuce leaves

walnut pieces

butter

cantaloupe

herbs

grapes

chicken

1 Preheat the oven to 400°F. Put the sprigs of tarragon or rosemary inside the chickens and season with salt and freshly ground black pepper. Tie the chickens in a neat shape with string. Spread the chickens with 4 tbsp of the softened butter, place in a roasting pan and pour round the stock. Cover loosely with foil and roast for about 1½ hours basting twice, until browned and the juices run clear. Remove the chickens from the roasting pan and leave to cool.

2 Add the wine to the roasting pan. Bring to a boil and cook until syrupy. Strain and leave to cool. Heat the remaining butter in a frying pan and gently fry the walnuts until lightly browned. Drain and cool. Scoop the melon into balls or into cubes. Joint the chickens.

3 To make the dressing, whisk the vinegar and oil together with a little salt and freshly ground black pepper. Remove all the fat from the chicken juices and add these to the dressing with the herbs. Adjust the seasoning.

4 Arrange the chicken pieces on a bed of lettuce, scatter over the grapes or stoned cherries, melon balls or cubes and spoon over the herb dressing. Sprinkle with toasted walnuts.

Chicken Roll

The roll can be prepared and cooked the day before and will freeze well too. Remove from the refrigerator about an hour before serving.

Serves 8

INGREDIENTS
1 × 4 lb chicken

FOR THE STUFFING
1 medium onion, finely chopped
4 tbsp melted butter
12 oz lean ground pork
4 rashers lean bacon, chopped
1 tbsp chopped fresh parsley
2 tsp chopped fresh thyme
2 cups fresh white bread crumbs
2 tbsp sherry
1 large egg, beaten
¼ cup shelled unsalted pistachio nuts
¼ cup pitted black olives (about 12)
salt and freshly ground black pepper

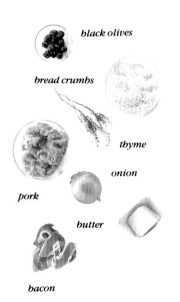

black olives

bread crumbs

thyme

onion

pork

butter

bacon

1 To make the stuffing, cook the chopped onion gently in 2 tbsp of the butter until soft. Turn into a bowl and cool. Add the remaining ingredients, mix thoroughly and season with salt and freshly ground black pepper.

2 To bone the chicken, use a small, sharp knife to remove the wing tips (pinions). Turn the chicken onto its breast and cut a line down the back bone.

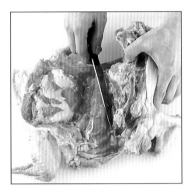

3 Cut the flesh away from the carcass, scraping the bones clean. Carefully cut through the sinew around the leg and wing joints and scrape down the bones to free them. Remove the carcass, taking care not to cut through the skin along the breast bone.

4 To stuff the chicken, lay it flat, skin side down and level the flesh as much as possible. Shape the stuffing down the center of the chicken and fold the sides over the stuffing.

5 Sew the flesh neatly together, using a needle and dark thread. Tie with fine string into a roll.

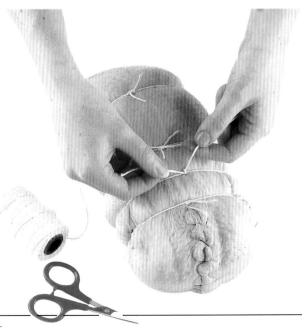

COOK'S TIPS

Thaw the chicken roll from frozen for 12 hours in the refrigerator, and leave to stand at cool room temperature for an hour before serving.

Use dark thread for sewing, as it is much easier to see so that you can remove it once the roll is cooked.

6 Preheat the oven to 350°F. Place the roll, with the join underneath, on a roasting rack in a roasting pan and brush generously with the remaining butter. Bake uncovered for about 1¼ hours or until cooked. Baste the chicken often with the juices in the roasting pan. Leave to cool completely before removing the string and thread. Wrap in foil and chill until ready for serving or freezing.

Stuffed Chicken Wings

These tasty tidbits can be served hot or cold at a buffet. They can be prepared and frozen in advance.

Makes 12

INGREDIENTS
12 large chicken wings

FOR THE FILLING
1 tsp cornstarch
¼ tsp salt
½ tsp fresh thyme
pinch of freshly ground black pepper

FOR THE COATING
2 cups dried bread crumbs
2 tbsp sesame seeds
2 eggs, beaten
oil, for deep-frying

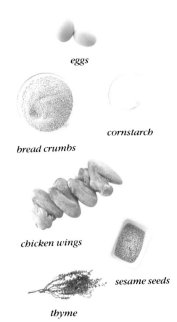

eggs

cornstarch

bread crumbs

chicken wings

sesame seeds

thyme

1 Remove the wing tips (pinions) and discard or use them for making stock. Skin the second joint sections, removing the two small bones and reserve the meat for the filling.

2 Grind the reserved meat and mix with the filling ingredients.

3 Holding the large end of the bone on the third section of the wing and using a sharp knife, cut the skin and flesh away from the bone, scraping down and pulling the meat over the small end forming a pocket. Repeat this process with the remaining wing sections.

4 Fill the tiny pockets with the filling. Mix the dried bread crumbs and the sesame seeds together. Place the bread crumb mixture and the beaten egg in separate dishes.

5 Brush the meat with beaten egg and roll in bread crumbs to cover. Chill and repeat to give a second layer, forming a thick coating. Chill until ready to fry.

6 Preheat the oven to 350°F. Heat 2 in of oil in a heavy-based pan until hot but not smoking or the bread crumbs will burn. Gently fry two or three chicken wings at a time until golden brown, remove and drain on paper towels. Complete the cooking in the preheated oven for about 15–20 minutes or until the meat is tender.

Chicken Lasagne

Based on the Italian beef lasagne, this is an excellent dish for entertaining guests of all ages. Serve simply with a green salad.

Serves 8

INGREDIENTS
2 tbsp olive oil
2 lb ground raw chicken
8 oz lean bacon rashers, chopped
2 garlic cloves, crushed
4 cups trimmed, sliced leeks
2 cups diced carrots
2 tbsp tomato paste
1⅞ cups fresh or canned chicken
    stock
12 sheets (no need to pre-cook)
    lasagne verde

FOR THE CHEESE SAUCE
4 tbsp butter
½ cup all-purpose flour
2½ cups milk
1 cup grated sharp Cheddar cheese
¼ tsp dry English mustard powder
salt and freshly ground black pepper

Cheddar cheese

lasagne verde

1 Heat the oil in a large flameproof casserole dish and brown the ground chicken and bacon briskly, separating the pieces with a wooden spoon. Add the crushed garlic cloves, chopped leeks and diced carrots and cook for 5 minutes until softened. Add the tomato paste, stock and seasoning. Bring to a boil, cover and simmer for 30 minutes.

2 For the sauce, melt the butter in a saucepan, add the flour and gradually blend in the milk, stirring until smooth. Bring to a boil, stirring all the time until thickened and simmer for several minutes. Add half the grated cheese and the mustard and season to taste.

3 Preheat the oven to 375°F. Layer the chicken mixture, lasagne and half the cheese sauce in a greased 5 pint oven-proof dish, starting and finishing with a layer of chicken.

4 Pour the remaining half of the cheese sauce over the top to cover, sprinkle over the remaining cheese and bake in the preheated oven for 1 hour, or until bubbling and lightly browned on top.

Chicken and Stilton Pies

A tasty filling of chicken and Stilton is wrapped in a crisp pastry crust to make four individual pies. They can be served hot or cold.

Makes 4

INGREDIENTS
3 cups self-rising flour
½ tsp salt
6 tbsp lard
6 tbsp butter
5 tbsp cold water
beaten egg, to glaze

FOR THE FILLING
1 lb boned and skinned chicken thighs
¼ cup chopped walnuts
1 oz scallions, sliced
½ cup Stilton, crumbled
1 oz celery, finely chopped
½ tsp dried thyme
salt and freshly ground black pepper

scallions

butter

celery   *Stilton*

thyme

flour

chicken thighs

1 Preheat the oven to 400°F. Mix the flour and salt in a bowl. Rub in the lard and butter with your fingers until the mixture resembles fine bread crumbs. Using a knife to cut and stir, mix in the cold water to form a stiff, pliable dough. Chill for 1 hour if possible.

2 Turn out onto a worktop and knead lightly until smooth. Divide into four equal pieces and roll out each piece to a thickness of ¼ in, keeping a good round shape. Cut into an 8 in circle, using a plate as a guide.

3 Remove any fat from the chicken thighs and cut into small cubes. Mix with the walnuts, scallions, Stilton, celery, thyme and seasoning and divide between the four pastry circles.

4 Brush the edge of the pastry with beaten egg and fold over, pinching and crimping the edges together well. Place on a greased baking sheet and bake in the preheated oven for about 45 minutes or until golden brown.

Chicken Bobotie

Perfect for a buffet party, this mild curry dish is set with savory custard, which makes serving easy. Serve with boiled rice and chutney.

Serves 8

INGREDIENTS
two thick slices white bread
1⅞ cups milk
2 tbsp olive oil
2 medium onions, finely chopped
2½ tbsp medium curry powder
2½ lb ground raw chicken
1 tbsp apricot jam, chutney or
    superfine sugar
2 tbsp wine vinegar or lemon juice
3 large eggs, beaten
⅓ cup raisins or sultanas
12 whole almonds
salt and freshly ground black pepper

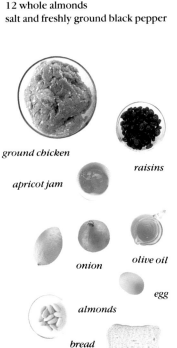

ground chicken

raisins

apricot jam

onion

olive oil

egg

almonds

bread

curry powder

1 Preheat the oven to 350°F. Soak the bread in ⅔ cup of the milk. Heat the oil in a frying pan and gently fry the onions until tender. Add the curry powder and continue to cook, stirring occasionally, for a further 2 minutes.

2 Add the ground chicken and brown all over, separating the grains of meat as they brown. Remove from the heat, season with salt and freshly ground black pepper, add the apricot jam, chutney or sugar and vinegar or lemon juice.

3 Mash the bread in the milk and add to the pan together with one of the beaten eggs and the raisins.

4 Grease a 2½ pint shallow ovenproof dish with butter. Spoon in the chicken mixture and level the top. Cover with buttered foil and bake for 30 minutes.

5 Meanwhile, beat the remaining eggs with the rest of the milk. Remove the dish from the oven and lower the temperature to 300°F. Break up the meat using two forks and pour over the beaten egg mixture.

6 Scatter the almonds over the top and return to the oven to bake, uncovered, for 30 minutes until set and golden brown all over.

Sweet and Sour Kebabs

This marinade contains sugar and will burn very easily, so grill the kebabs slowly, turning often. Serve with Harlequin Rice.

Serves 4

INGREDIENTS
2 boned and skinned chicken breasts
8 pickling onions or 2 medium
    onions, peeled
4 lean bacon rashers
3 firm bananas
1 red pepper, seeded and diced

FOR THE MARINADE
2 tbsp brown sugar
1 tbsp Worcestershire sauce
2 tbsp lemon juice
salt and freshly ground black pepper

FOR THE HARLEQUIN RICE
2 tbsp olive oil
generous 1 cup cooked rice
1 cup cooked peas
1 small red pepper, seeded and diced

pepper

Worcestershire
sauce

lemon

bacon

onions

sugar

bananas

chicken breast

1 Mix together the marinade ingredients. Cut each chicken breast into four pieces, add to the marinade, cover and leave for at least four hours or preferably overnight.

2 Peel the pickling onions, blanch them in boiling water for 5 minutes and drain. If using medium onions, quarter them after blanching.

3 Cut each rasher of bacon in half. Peel the bananas and cut each into three pieces. Wrap a rasher of bacon around each piece of banana.

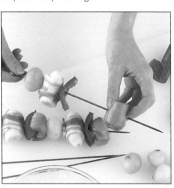

4 Thread onto metal skewers with the chicken pieces, onions and pepper pieces. Brush with the marinade.

5 Broil or barbecue over low coals for 15 minutes, turning and basting frequently with the marinade. Keep warm while you prepare the rice.

COOK'S TIP
Pour boiling water over the small onions and then drain, to make peeling easier.

6 Heat the oil in a frying pan and add the rice, peas and diced pepper. Stir the mixture until heated through and serve with the kebabs.

Chicken Liver Kebabs

These may be barbecued outdoors and served with salad and baked potatoes, or broiled indoors and served with rice and broccoli.

Serves 4

INGREDIENTS
4 oz (roughly 6) lean bacon rashers
12 oz trimmed chicken livers
12 large, ready-to-eat pitted prunes
12 cherry tomatoes
8 button mushrooms
2 tbsp olive oil

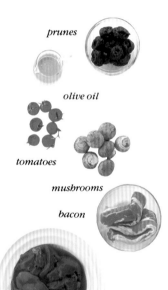

prunes

olive oil

tomatoes

mushrooms

bacon

chicken livers

1 Cut each rasher of bacon into two pieces, wrap a piece around each chicken liver and secure in position with wooden toothpicks.

2 Wrap the pitted prunes around the cherry tomatoes.

3 Thread the bacon-wrapped livers onto metal skewers with the tomatoes and prunes. Brush with oil. Cover the tomatoes and prunes with foil to protect them while broiling or barbecuing. Cook for 5 minutes on each side.

4 Remove the toothpicks and serve the kebabs immediately.

Citrus Kebabs

Serve on a bed of lettuce leaves and garnish with fresh mint and orange and lemon slices.

Serves 4

INGREDIENTS
4 chicken breasts, skinned and boned
fresh mint sprigs, to garnish
orange, lemon or lime slices, to
    garnish (optional)

FOR THE MARINADE
finely grated rind and juice of
    ½ orange
finely grated rind and juice of ½ small
    lemon or lime
2 tbsp olive oil
2 tbsp honey
2 tbsp chopped fresh mint
¼ tsp ground cumin
salt and freshly ground black pepper

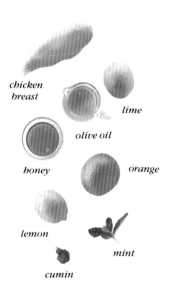

chicken breast
lime
olive oil
honey
orange
lemon
mint
cumin

1 Cut the chicken into cubes of approximately 1 in.

2 Mix the marinade ingredients together, add the chicken cubes and leave to marinade for at least 2 hours.

3 Thread the chicken pieces onto skewers and broil or barbecue over low coals for 15 minutes, basting with the marinade and turning frequently. Serve garnished with extra mint and citrus slices if desired.

Chicken Liver Salad

This salad may be served as a first course on individual plates.

Serves 4

INGREDIENTS
mixed salad leaves, e.g. frisée and
 oakleaf lettuce or radicchio
1 avocado, diced
2 pink grapefruits, segmented
12 oz trimmed chicken livers
2 tbsp olive oil
1 garlic clove, crushed
salt and freshly ground black pepper
crusty bread, to serve

FOR THE DRESSING
2 tbsp lemon juice
4 tbsp olive oil
½ tsp whole grain mustard
½ tsp honey
1 tbsp snipped fresh chives

chicken livers

grapefruit

olive oil

honey

avocado

mustard

lemon

chives

salad leaves

garlic

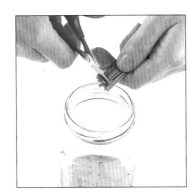

1 First prepare the dressing: put all the ingredients into a screw-topped jar and shake vigorously to emulsify. Taste and adjust the seasoning.

2 Wash and dry the salad. Arrange attractively on a serving plate with the avocado and grapefruit.

3 Dry the chicken livers on paper towels and remove any unwanted pieces. Cut the larger livers in half and leave the smaller ones whole.

4 Heat the oil in a large frying pan. Stir-fry the livers and garlic briskly until the livers are brown all over (they should be slightly pink inside).

5 Season with salt and freshly ground black pepper and drain on paper towels.

6 Place the liver on the salad and spoon over the dressing. Serve immediately with warm crusty bread.

Chicken Satay

Marinade in the satay sauce overnight to allow the flavors to penetrate the chicken. Soak wooden skewers in water overnight to prevent them from burning while cooking.

Serves 4

INGREDIENTS
4 chicken breasts
lettuce leaves, to serve
scallions, to serve
lemon slices, to garnish

FOR THE SATAY
½ cup chunky peanut butter
1 small onion, chopped
1 garlic clove, crushed
2 tbsp chutney
4 tbsp olive oil
1 tsp light soy sauce
2 tbsp lemon juice
¼ tsp chili powder or cayenne
   pepper

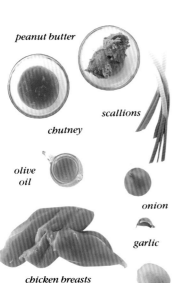

peanut butter

scallions

chutney

olive oil

onion

garlic

chicken breasts

lemon

1 Put all the satay ingredients into a food processor and blend until smooth. Spoon into a large dish.

2 Remove all bone and skin from the chicken and cut into 1 in cubes. Add to the satay mixture and stir to coat the chicken pieces. Cover with plastic wrap and refrigerate for at least 4 hours or, better still, overnight.

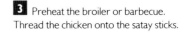

3 Preheat the broiler or barbecue. Thread the chicken onto the satay sticks.

4 Cook for 10 minutes, brushing occasionally with the satay sauce. Serve on a bed of lettuce with scallions and garnish with lemon slices.

Chicken and Pasta Salad

This is a delicious way to use up left-over cooked chicken, and makes a filling meal.

Serves 4

INGREDIENTS
8 oz tri-colored pasta twists
2 tbsp bottled pesto sauce
1 tbsp olive oil
1 beefsteak tomato
12 pitted black olives
8 oz cooked green beans
12 oz cooked chicken, cubed
salt and freshly ground black pepper
fresh basil, to garnish

tomato

green
beans

olive oil

pesto sauce

basil

pasta twists

chicken

black olives

1 Cook the pasta in plenty of boiling, salted water until *al dente* (for about 12 minutes or as directed on the package).

2 Drain the pasta and rinse in plenty of cold running water. Put into a bowl and stir in the pesto sauce and olive oil.

3 Skin the tomato by placing in boiling water for about 10 seconds and then into cold water, to loosen the skin.

4 Cut the tomato into small cubes and add to the pasta with the black olives, seasoning and green beans cut into 1½ in lengths. Add the cubed chicken. Toss gently together and transfer to a serving platter. Garnish with fresh basil.

Dijon Chicken Salad

An attractive and elegant dish to serve for lunch with herb and garlic bread.

Serves 4

INGREDIENTS
4 boned and skinned chicken breasts
mixed salad leaves, e.g. watercress
    and oakleaf lettuce, to serve

FOR THE MARINADE
2 tbsp Dijon mustard
3 garlic cloves, crushed
1 tbsp grated onion
4 tbsp white wine

FOR THE MUSTARD DRESSING
2 tbsp tarragon wine vinegar
1 tsp Dijon mustard
1 tsp honey
6 tbsp olive oil
salt and freshly ground black pepper

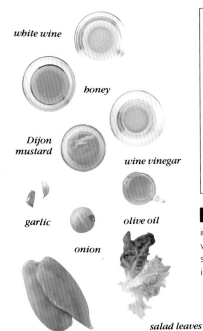

white wine

honey

Dijon mustard

wine vinegar

garlic   *olive oil*

onion

salad leaves

chicken breasts

1 Mix all the marinade ingredients together in a shallow glass or earthenware dish that is large enough to hold the chicken in a single layer.

2 Turn the chicken over in the marinade to coat completely, cover with plastic wrap and then chill in the refrigerator overnight.

3 Preheat the oven to 375°F. Transfer the chicken and the marinade into an ovenproof dish, cover with foil and bake for about 35 minutes or until tender. Leave to cool in the liquid.

4 Put all the mustard dressing ingredients into a screw-topped jar, shake vigorously to emulsify, and adjust the seasoning. (This can be made several days in advance and stored in the refrigerator.)

5 Slice the chicken thinly, fan out the slices and arrange on a serving dish with the salad leaves.

6 Spoon over some of the mustard dressing and serve.

Deviled Drumsticks

Marinate the drumsticks overnight for maximum flavor. Broil or barbecue them and serve with yellow rice and tomato, bean and onion salad.

Serves 4

INGREDIENTS
8 large chicken drumsticks

FOR THE DRY MARINADE
2 tsp salt
2 tsp superfine sugar
1 tsp freshly ground black pepper
1 tsp ground ginger
1 tsp dry English mustard powder
1 tsp paprika
2 tbsp olive oil

FOR THE SAUCE
2 tbsp tomato catsup
1 tbsp mushroom catsup
1 tbsp chili sauce
1 tbsp soy sauce
1 tbsp fruit sauce

FOR THE YELLOW RICE
2 tbsp butter
1 medium onion, finely chopped
1 tsp ground turmeric
generous 1 cup cooked rice

1 Mix all the dry marinade ingredients together with the olive oil.

2 Rub into the drumsticks, cover with plastic wrap and leave for at least 1 hour, or preferably overnight.

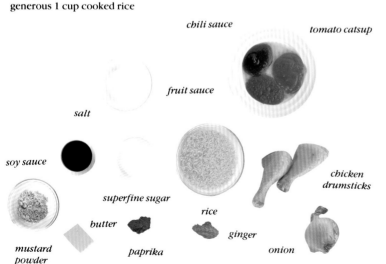

chili sauce
tomato catsup
fruit sauce
salt
soy sauce
chicken drumsticks
superfine sugar
rice
butter
ginger
mustard powder
paprika
onion

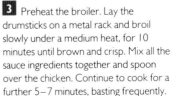

3 Preheat the broiler. Lay the drumsticks on a metal rack and broil slowly under a medium heat, for 10 minutes until brown and crisp. Mix all the sauce ingredients together and spoon over the chicken. Continue to cook for a further 5–7 minutes, basting frequently.

4 For the yellow rice, heat the butter in a large pan, add the onion and cook until tender. Add the turmeric and cook for a further minute.

5 Add the cooked rice and stir to reheat. Spoon onto a serving plate and arrange the deviled drumsticks on top.

Tandoori Chicken

A popular party dish. The chicken is marinated the night before so all you have to do on the day is to cook it in a very hot oven and serve with wedges of lemon and green salad.

Serves 4

INGREDIENTS
1 × 3½ lb chicken, cut into 8 pieces
juice of 1 large lemon
⅔ cup plain low fat yogurt
3 garlic cloves, crushed
2 tbsp olive oil
1 tsp ground turmeric
2 tsp ground paprika
1 tsp grated fresh ginger root or
   ½ tsp ground ginger
2 tsp garam masala
1 tsp salt
a few drops of red food coloring
   (optional)

lemon

olive oil

garlic

ginger

yogurt

garam masala

chicken

paprika

turmeric

1 Skin the chicken pieces and cut two slits in each piece.

2 Arrange in a single layer in a dish and pour over the lemon juice.

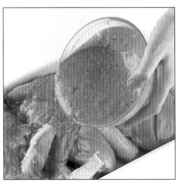

3 Mix together the remaining ingredients and pour the sauce over the chicken pieces, turning them to coat thoroughly. Cover with plastic wrap and chill overnight.

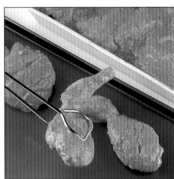

4 Preheat the oven to 425°F. Remove the chicken from the marinade and arrange in a single layer in a shallow baking sheet. Bake for 15 minutes, turn over, and cook for a further 15 minutes or until tender.

Chinese Chicken Wings

These are best eaten with fingers as a first course, so make sure you provide finger bowls and plenty of paper napkins.

Serves 4

INGREDIENTS
12 chicken wings
3 garlic cloves, crushed
2 tsp grated fresh ginger root
juice of 1 large lemon
3 tbsp soy sauce
3 tbsp honey
½ tsp chili powder
⅔ cup fresh or canned chicken stock
salt and fresh ground black pepper
lemon wedges, to garnish

garlic

lemon

chicken wings

soy sauce

honey   *chili powder*

ginger

1 Remove the wing tips (pinions) and use to make the stock. Cut the wings into two joints.

2 Mix the remaining ingredients together and coat the chicken pieces in the mixture completely. Cover with plastic wrap and marinate overnight.

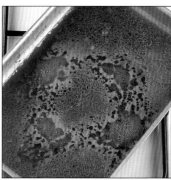

3 Preheat the oven to 425°F. Remove the wings from the marinade and arrange in a single layer in a roasting pan. Bake for 20–25 minutes, basting at least twice with the marinade during cooking until all the marinade is used up.

4 Place the wings on a serving plate. Add the stock to the marinade in the roasting pan, and bring to a boil. Cook to a syrupy consistency and spoon a little over the wings. Serve garnished with lemon wedges.

Chicken Biriani

This is a good dish for entertaining. It can be prepared in advance and reheated in the oven. Serve with traditional curry accompaniments.

Serves 8

INGREDIENTS
2 lb boneless chicken thighs
4 tbsp olive oil
2 large onions, thinly sliced
1–2 green chilies, seeded and finely
　chopped
1 tsp grated fresh ginger root
1 garlic clove, crushed
1 tbsp hot curry powder
2/3 cup fresh or canned chicken stock
2/3 cup plain low fat yogurt
2 tbsp chopped fresh coriander
salt and freshly ground black pepper

FOR THE SPICED RICE
1 lb basmati rice
1/2 tsp garam masala
3 3/4 cups fresh or canned chicken
　stock or water
1/3 cup raisins or sultanas
1/4 cup toasted almonds

ginger

basmati rice

curry powder

chilies

yogurt

coriander

chicken thighs

almonds

Cover with buttered foil and bake in the oven for 30 minutes to reheat.

1 Put the basmati rice into a sieve and wash under cold running water to remove any starchy powder coating the grains. Then put into a bowl and cover with cold water and soak for 30 minutes. The grains will absorb some water so that they will not stick together in a solid mass while cooking.

2 Preheat the oven to 325°F. Cut the chicken into even-sized cubes, each approximately 1 in square. Heat half the oil in a large flameproof casserole, add one onion and cook until softened but not browned. Add the finely chopped chilies, ginger, garlic and curry powder and cook for a further 2 minutes, stirring occasionally.

3 Add the stock and seasoning, bring to a boil and add the chicken pieces. Cover and continue cooking in the oven for about 20 minutes or until tender.

4 Remove from the oven and then stir in the yogurt.

5 Meanwhile, heat the remaining oil in a flameproof casserole and cook the remaining onion gently until tender and lightly browned. Add the drained rice, garam masala and stock or water. Bring to a boil, cover and cook in the oven with the chicken for 25–35 minutes or until tender and the stock has been absorbed.

6 To serve, stir the raisins or sultanas and toasted almonds into the rice. Spoon half the rice into a large deep serving dish, cover with the chicken and then the remaining rice. Sprinkle with chopped coriander to garnish.

Chicken Tikka

The red food coloring gives this dish its traditional bright color. Serve with lemon wedges and a crisp mixed salad.

Serves 4

INGREDIENTS
1 × 3½ lb chicken
mixed salad leaves, e.g. frisée and
    oakleaf lettuce or radicchio,
    to serve

FOR THE MARINADE
⅔ cup plain low fat yogurt
1 tsp ground paprika
2 tsp grated fresh ginger root
1 garlic clove, crushed
2 tsp garam masala
½ tsp salt
red food coloring (optional)
juice of 1 lemon

lemon

chicken

salt

yogurt

paprika

garlic   ginger

1 Joint the chicken and cut it into eight pieces, using a sharp knife.

2 Mix all the marinade ingredients in a container large enough to hold the chicken pieces. Add the chicken, coat well and chill for 4 hours or overnight to allow the flavors to penetrate the flesh.

garam masala

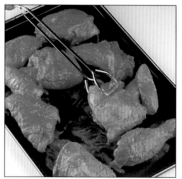

3 Preheat the oven to 400°F. Remove the chicken pieces from the marinade and arrange them in a single layer in a large ovenproof dish. Bake for 30–40 minutes or until tender.

4 Baste with a little of the marinade while cooking. Arrange on a bed of salad leaves and serve hot or cold.

Chili Chicken

Serve as a simple supper dish with boiled potatoes and broccoli, or as a party dish with rice.

Serves 4

INGREDIENTS
12 chicken thighs
1 tbsp olive oil
1 medium onion, thinly sliced
1 garlic clove, crushed
1 tsp chili powder or 1 fresh chili, chopped
1 × 14 oz can chopped tomatoes, with their juice
1 tsp superfine sugar
1 × 15 oz can red kidney beans, drained
salt and freshly ground black pepper

red kidney beans

tomatoes

onion

olive oil

garlic

chicken thighs

superfine sugar

chili powder

1 Cut the chicken into large cubes, removing all skin and bones. Heat the oil in a large flameproof casserole and brown the chicken pieces on all sides. Remove and keep warm.

2 Add the onion and garlic clove to the casserole and cook gently until tender. Stir in the chili powder or chopped fresh chili and cook for 2 minutes. Add the can of tomatoes with their juice, seasoning and sugar. Bring to a boil.

3 Replace the chicken pieces, cover the casserole and simmer for about 30 minutes until tender.

4 Add the red kidney beans and gently cook for a further 5 minutes to heat them through before serving.

Simple Chicken Curry

Curry powder can be bought in three different strengths – mild, medium and hot. Use the type you prefer to suit your taste.

Serves 4

INGREDIENTS
8 chicken legs (thighs and
   drumsticks)
2 tbsp olive oil
1 onion, thinly sliced
1 garlic clove, crushed
1 tbsp medium curry powder
1 tbsp all-purpose flour
1⅞ cups fresh or canned chicken
   stock
1 beefsteak tomato
1 tbsp mango chutney
1 tbsp lemon juice
salt and freshly ground black pepper
2½ cups boiled rice, to serve

chicken

lemon

olive oil

garlic

onion

flour

tomato

mango chutney

curry powder

1 Cut the chicken legs in half. Heat the oil in a large flameproof casserole and brown all the chicken on both sides. Remove and keep warm.

2 Add the onion and garlic clove to the casserole and cook until tender. Add the curry powder and cook gently for 2 minutes.

3 Add the flour, and gradually blend in the stock and the seasoning.

4 Bring to a boil, replace the chicken pieces, cover and simmer for 20–30 minutes or until tender.

5 Skin the tomato by blanching in boiling water for 15 seconds, then run under cold water to loosen the skin. Peel and cut into small cubes.

6 Add to the chicken, with the mango chutney and lemon juice. Heat through gently and adjust the seasoning to taste. Serve with plenty of boiled rice and Indian accompaniments.

Crunchy Stuffed Chicken Breasts

These can be prepared ahead of time as long as the stuffing is quite cold before the chicken is stuffed. It is an ideal dish for entertaining.

Serves 4

INGREDIENTS
4 boned chicken breasts
2 tbsp butter
1 garlic clove, crushed
1 tbsp Dijon mustard

FOR THE STUFFING
1 tbsp butter
1 bunch scallions, sliced
3 tbsp fresh bread crumbs
2 tbsp pine nuts
1 egg yolk
1 tbsp chopped fresh parsley
salt and freshly ground black pepper
4 tbsp grated cheese

FOR THE TOPPING
2 bacon rashers, finely chopped
1 cup fresh bread crumbs
1 tbsp grated Parmesan cheese
1 tbsp chopped fresh parsley

bread crumbs   *cheese*   *egg yolk*

bacon

mustard

parsley

pine nuts

chicken breasts

1 Preheat the oven to 400°F. To make the stuffing, heat 1 tbsp of the butter in a frying pan and cook the scallions over a medium heat, stirring frequently, until they are soft. Remove from the heat and allow to cool for a few minutes.

2 Add the remaining ingredients and mix thoroughly.

3 To make the topping, fry the chopped bacon until crispy, drain and add to the bread crumbs, Parmesan cheese and fresh parsley.

4 Carefully cut a pocket in each chicken breast, using a sharp knife.

5 Divide the stuffing into four and use to fill the pockets. Transfer to a buttered ovenproof dish.

6 Melt the remaining butter, mix it with the crushed garlic and mustard, and brush liberally over the chicken. Press on the topping and bake uncovered for about 20–30 minutes, or until tender.

Apricot and Chicken Casserole

A mild curry and fruity chicken dish served with almond rice. This makes a good winter meal.

Serves 4

INGREDIENTS
1 tbsp oil
8 large boned and skinned chicken thighs, cut into 4 pieces
1 medium onion, finely chopped
1 tsp medium curry powder
2 tbsp all-purpose flour
1⅞ cups fresh or canned chicken stock
juice of 1 large orange
8 ready-to-eat dried apricots, halved
1 tbsp sultanas
salt and freshly ground black pepper

FOR THE ALMOND RICE
2 cups cooked rice
1 tbsp butter
½ cup toasted almonds

almonds

onion

chicken thighs

sultanas

orange

curry powder

flour

rice

apricots

1 Preheat the oven to 350°F. Heat the oil in a large frying pan. Cut the chicken into even-sized cubes and then brown them quickly all over in the oil. Add the chopped onion and cook gently until soft and lightly browned.

2 Transfer to a large flameproof casserole, sprinkle in the curry powder and cook again for a few minutes. Add the flour and blend in the stock and orange juice. Bring to a boil and season with salt and freshly ground black pepper.

3 Add the apricots and sultanas, cover with a lid and cook gently for an hour, or until tender, in the preheated oven. Adjust the seasoning to taste.

4 To make the almond rice, reheat the pre-cooked rice with the butter and season to taste. Stir in the toasted almonds just before serving.

Coq au Vin

There are many variations of this traditional French dish, but this one is especially delicious. Serve it with warm French bread.

Serves 4

INGREDIENTS
2 tbsp olive oil
1 tbsp butter
1 × 3½ lb chicken, cut into 8 pieces
4 oz smoked ham, cut into ¼ in strips
4 oz pearl onions, peeled
4 oz button mushrooms
2 garlic cloves, crushed
2 tbsp brandy
scant 1 cup red wine
1¼ cups fresh or canned chicken stock
1 bouquet garni
1 tbsp butter, blended with 2 tbsp flour
salt and freshly ground black pepper
chopped parsley to garnish

parsley

chicken

mushrooms

olive oil

garlic

butter

ham

chicken stock

bouquet garni

1 Preheat the oven to 325°F. Heat the oil and butter in a large flameproof casserole and brown the chicken pieces on both sides.

2 Add the ham strips, peeled onions, mushrooms and garlic cloves.

3 Pour over the brandy and set it alight. Pour over the red wine, stock, bouquet garni and seasoning. Cover and cook slowly for about 1 hour, either on top of the stove or in the preheated oven.

4 Remove the chicken and keep warm. Thicken the sauce with the butter mixture and season to taste. Cook for several minutes and replace the chicken. Sprinkle with chopped parsley and serve.

Koftas in Tomato Sauce

Delicious meatballs in a rich tomato sauce. Serve with pasta shapes and grated Parmesan cheese if desired.

Serves 4

INGREDIENTS
1½ lb boneless chicken
1 onion, grated
1 garlic clove, crushed
1 tbsp chopped fresh parsley
½ tsp ground cumin
½ tsp ground coriander
1 egg, beaten
seasoned flour, for rolling
4 tbsp olive oil
salt and freshly ground black pepper
chopped fresh parsley, to garnish

FOR THE TOMATO SAUCE
1 tbsp butter
1 tbsp all-purpose flour
1 cup fresh or canned chicken stock
1 × 14 oz can chopped tomatoes
1 tsp superfine sugar
¼ tsp dried mixed herbs

superfine sugar
onion
dried herbs
olive oil
tomatoes
flour
ground chicken
spices
parsley
garlic

1 Preheat the oven to 350°F. Remove any skin and bone from the chicken and grind or chop it finely.

2 Put into a bowl together with the onion, garlic clove, parsley, spices, seasoning and beaten egg.

3 Mix together thoroughly and shape into 24 × 1½ in balls. Roll lightly in seasoned flour.

4 Heat the oil in a frying pan and brown the balls in small batches (this keeps the oil temperature hot and prevents the flour becoming soggy). Remove and drain on paper towels. There is no need to cook the balls any further at this stage as they will cook in the tomato sauce.

5 For the tomato sauce, melt the butter in a large saucepan. Add the flour, and then blend in the stock and tomatoes along with their juice. Add the sugar and herbs. Bring to a boil, cover and simmer for 10–15 minutes.

6 Place the browned chicken balls into a shallow ovenproof dish and pour over the tomato sauce, cover with foil and bake in the preheated oven for 30–40 minutes. Adjust the seasoning to taste and sprinkle with parsley.

Chicken in Creamed Horseradish

The piquant flavor of the horseradish sauce gives this quick dish a sophisticated taste. Use half the quantity if using fresh horseradish.

Serves 4

INGREDIENTS
2 tbsp olive oil
4 chicken joints
2 tbsp butter
2 tbsp all-purpose flour
1⅞ cups fresh or canned chicken stock
2 tbsp creamed horseradish sauce
salt and freshly ground black pepper
1 tbsp chopped fresh parsley

flour

chicken

horseradish sauce

butter

parsley

1 Heat the oil in a large flameproof casserole and gently brown the chicken joints on both sides over a medium heat. Remove the chicken from the casserole and keep warm.

2 Wipe out the casserole, melt the butter, stir in the flour and blend in the stock gradually. Bring to a boil, stirring all the time.

3 Add the horseradish sauce and season with salt and freshly ground black pepper. Return the chicken to the casserole, cover and simmer for 30–40 minutes or until tender.

4 Transfer to a serving dish and sprinkle with fresh parsley. Serve with mashed potatoes and green beans if desired.

...ecipe. Any
... mussels and
...an.

to 350°F. Cut the

... paella pan or
... e and brown the
... les. Add the
onion and garlic and stir in the turmeric.
Cook for 2 minutes.

pepper

long grain rice

chicken

3 Slice the sausage or dice the ham and
add to the pan, with the rice and stock.
Bring to a boil and season to taste, cover
and bake for 15 minutes.

4 Remove and add the chopped
tomatoes and sliced red pepper and
frozen peas. Return to the oven and cook
for a further 10–15 minutes or until the
chicken is tender and the rice has
absorbed the stock.

Parmesan Chicken Bake

The tomato sauce may be made the day before and left to cool. Serve with crusty bread and salad.

Serves 4

INGREDIENTS
4 boned and skinned chicken breasts
4 tbsp all-purpose flour
4 tbsp olive oil
salt and freshly ground black pepper

FOR THE TOMATO SAUCE
1 tbsp olive oil
1 onion, finely chopped
1 stalk celery, finely chopped
1 red pepper, seeded and diced
1 garlic clove, crushed
1 × 14 oz can chopped tomatoes
⅔ cup fresh or canned chicken stock
1 tbsp tomato paste
2 tsp superfine sugar
1 tbsp chopped basil
1 tbsp chopped parsley

TO ASSEMBLE
8 oz mozzarella cheese, sliced
4 tbsp grated Parmesan cheese
2 tbsp fresh bread crumbs

chicken breasts
tomatoes
onion
garlic
olive oil
Parmesan
tomato paste
celery
mozzarella
flour
bread crumbs
parsley
pepper
basil

1 First make the tomato sauce. Heat 1 tbsp of the oil in a frying pan and gently cook the onion, celery, pepper and garlic clove in the oil until tender.

2 Add the tomatoes with their juice, the stock, paste, sugar and herbs. Season to taste and bring to a boil. Simmer for 30 minutes until thick, stirring occasionally.

3 Divide each chicken breast into two natural fillets, place between sheets of plastic wrap and flatten to a thickness of ¼ in with a rolling pin.

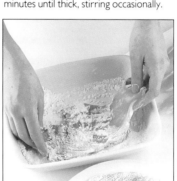

4 Season the flour with salt and pepper. Toss the chicken breasts in the flour to coat, shaking to remove the excess.

5 Preheat the oven to 350°F. Heat the remaining oil in a large frying pan and then cook the chicken quickly in batches for about 3–4 minutes until colored. Remove and keep warm while frying the rest of the chicken.

6 To assemble, layer the chicken pieces with the cheeses and thick tomato sauce, finishing with a layer of cheese and bread crumbs. Bake uncovered for 20–30 minutes or until golden brown.

Chicken Stroganov

This is based on the classic Russian dish, usually made with fillet of beef. Serve with rice to which chopped celery, scallions and parsley have been added.

Serves 4

INGREDIENTS
4 large boned and skinned
   chicken breasts
3 tbsp olive oil
1 large onion, thinly sliced
8 oz mushrooms, sliced
1¼ cups sour cream
salt and freshly ground black pepper
1 tbsp chopped fresh parsley,
   to garnish

sour cream

onion

mushrooms

parsley

olive oil

chicken breasts

1 Divide each chicken breast into two natural fillets, place between two sheets of plastic wrap and flatten to a thickness of ¼ in with a rolling pin.

2 Cut the chicken into 1 in strips diagonally across the fillets.

3 Heat 2 tbsp oil in a large frying pan and cook the sliced onion slowly until soft but not colored.

4 Add the mushrooms and cook until golden brown. Remove and keep warm.

5 Increase the heat, add 15 the remaining oil and fry the chicken very quickly, in small batches, for 3–4 minutes until lightly colored. Remove and keep warm while frying the rest of the chicken.

COOK'S TIP
If sour cream is not available, fresh heavy cream may be used, soured with the juice of ½ a lemon.

6 Return all the chicken, onions and mushrooms to the pan and season with salt and freshly ground black pepper. Stir in the sour cream and bring to a boil. Sprinkle with fresh parsley and serve immediately.

Chicken Cordon Bleu

A rich dish, popular with cheese lovers. Serve simply with green beans and tiny baked potatoes, cut and filled with cream cheese.

Serves 4

INGREDIENTS
4 boned and skinned chicken breasts
4 slices cooked lean ham
4 tbsp grated Gruyère or Emmenthal cheese
2 tbsp olive oil
4 oz button mushrooms, sliced
4 tbsp white wine
salt and freshly ground black pepper
watercress, to garnish

white wine

olive oil

cheese

chicken breasts

ham

watercress

button mushrooms

1 Place the chicken between two pieces of plastic wrap and flatten to a thickness of ¼ in with a rolling pin. Place the chicken breasts, outer side down, on the board and lay a slice of ham on each. Divide the cheese between the chicken and season with a little salt and freshly ground black pepper.

2 Fold in half and secure with wooden toothpicks, making a large 'stitch' to hold the pieces together.

3 Heat the oil in a large frying pan and brown the chicken on both sides. Remove and keep warm.

4 Add the mushrooms to the pan and cook for several minutes to brown lightly. Replace the chicken and pour over the wine, cover, and cook gently for 15–20 minutes until tender. Remove the wooden toothpicks and arrange on a serving dish with a bunch of watercress.

Chicken in Herb Crusts

The chicken breasts can be brushed with melted butter instead of mustard before being coated in the bread crumb mixture. Serve with new potatoes and salad.

Serves 4

INGREDIENTS
4 boned and skinned chicken breasts
1 tbsp Dijon mustard
1 cup fresh bread crumbs
2 tbsp chopped fresh parsley
1 tbsp dried mixed herbs
2 tbsp butter, melted
salt and freshly ground black pepper

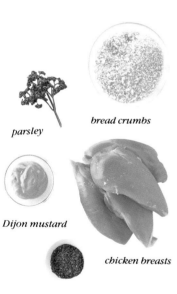

parsley

bread crumbs

Dijon mustard

chicken breasts

dried herbs

1 Preheat the oven to 350°F. Lay the chicken breasts in a greased ovenproof dish and spread them evenly with the Dijon mustard. Season with salt and freshly ground black pepper.

2 Mix the bread crumbs and herbs together thoroughly.

3 Press onto the chicken to coat. Spoon over the melted butter. Bake uncovered for 20 minutes or until tender and crisp.

Lemon Chicken Stir-fry

It is essential to prepare all the ingredients before you begin so they are ready to cook. This dish is cooked in minutes.

Serves 4

INGREDIENTS
4 boned and skinned chicken breasts
1 tbsp light soy sauce
5 tbsp cornstarch
1 bunch scallions
1 lemon
1 garlic clove, crushed
1 tbsp superfine sugar
2 tbsp sherry
2/3 cup fresh or canned chicken stock
4 tbsp olive oil
salt and freshly ground black pepper

superfine sugar

garlic

olive oil

scallions

lemon

soy sauce

cornstarch

chicken breasts

1 Divide the chicken breasts into two natural fillets. Place each between two sheets of plastic wrap and flatten to a thickness of 1/4 in with a rolling pin.

2 Cut into 1 in strips across the grain of the fillets. Put the chicken into a bowl with the soy sauce and toss to coat thoroughly, then sprinkle over 4 tbsp cornstarch to coat each piece.

3 Trim the roots off the scallions and cut diagonally into 1/2 in pieces. With a swivel peeler, remove the lemon rind in thin strips and cut into fine shreds. Reserve the lemon juice. Have ready the garlic clove, sugar, sherry, stock, lemon juice and the remaining cornstarch blended to a paste with cold water.

4 Heat the oil in a wok or large frying pan and cook the chicken very quickly in small batches for 3–4 minutes until lightly colored. Remove and keep warm while frying the rest of the chicken.

5 Add the scallions and garlic to the pan and cook for 2 minutes.

6 Add the remaining ingredients and bring to a boil, stirring until thickened. Add more sherry or stock if necessary and stir until the chicken is evenly covered with sauce. Reheat for 2 more minutes. Serve immediately.

Chicken with Mushrooms

Serve on a dish surrounded with nutty brown rice or tagliatelle verde. White wine or brandy may be used to deglaze the pan in place of sherry.

Serves 4

INGREDIENTS
4 large boned and skinned
    chicken breasts
3 tbsp olive oil
1 onion, thinly sliced
1 garlic clove, crushed
8 oz button mushrooms, quartered
2 tbsp sherry
1 tbsp lemon juice
⅔ cup light cream
salt and freshly ground black pepper

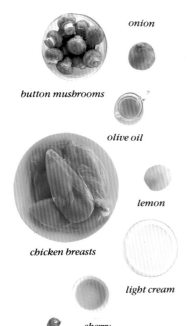

onion

button mushrooms

olive oil

lemon

chicken breasts

light cream

sherry

garlic

1 Divide the chicken breasts into two natural fillets. Place each between two sheets of plastic wrap and flatten to a thickness of ¼ in with a rolling pin. Cut into 1 in diagonal strips.

2 Heat 2 tbsp oil in a large frying pan and cook the onion and garlic clove slowly until tender.

3 Add the mushrooms and cook them for a further 5 minutes. Remove and keep warm.

4 Increase the heat. Add the remaining oil and fry the chicken very quickly, in small batches for 3–4 minutes until lightly colored. Season each batch with a little salt and freshly ground black pepper. Remove and keep warm while frying the rest of the chicken.

5 Add the sherry and lemon juice to the casserole and quickly return the chicken, onions, garlic and mushrooms, stirring to coat.

6 Stir in the cream and bring to a boil. Adjust the seasoning to taste. Serve immediately.

Spatchcock of Poussins

Allow one poussin or Rock Cornish game hen per person. Serve with boiled new potatoes and salad.

Serves 4

INGREDIENTS
4 poussins or Rock Cornish game hens
4 tbsp butter, melted
1 tbsp lemon juice
1 tbsp chopped fresh herbs, e.g. rosemary and parsley, plus extra to garnish
salt and freshly ground black pepper
lemon slices, to garnish

poussins

butter   *lemon*

1 Remove any trussing strings from the birds and using a pair of kitchen scissors, cut down on either side of the backbone. Lay the poussins flat and flatten with the help of a rolling pin or mallet.

2 Thread the legs and wings onto skewers to keep the poussins flat while they are cooking.

3 Brush both sides with melted butter and season to taste. Sprinkle with lemon juice and herbs.

4 Preheat the broiler to medium heat and cook skin-side first for 6 minutes until golden brown. Turn over, brush with butter and grill for a further 6–8 minutes or until cooked. Garnish with more chopped herbs and lemon slices.

Chicken with Asparagus

Canned asparagus may be used, but will not require cooking – simply add at the end to warm through.

Serves 4

INGREDIENTS

4 large boned and skinned
  chicken breasts
1 tbsp ground coriander
2 tbsp olive oil
20 slender asparagus spears, cut into
  3–4 in lengths
1¼ cups fresh or canned chicken
  stock
1 tbsp cornstarch
1 tbsp lemon juice
salt and freshly ground black pepper
1 tbsp chopped fresh parsley,
  to garnish

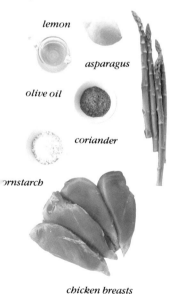

lemon

asparagus

olive oil

coriander

ornstarch

chicken breasts

1 Divide the chicken breasts into two natural fillets. Place each between two sheets of plastic wrap and flatten to a thickness of ¼ in with a rolling pin. Cut into 1 in strips diagonally across the fillets. Sprinkle over the ground coriander and toss to coat each piece.

2 Heat the oil in a large frying pan and fry the chicken very quickly in small batches for 3–4 minutes until lightly colored. Season each batch with a little salt and freshly ground black pepper. Remove and keep warm while frying the rest of the chicken.

3 Add the asparagus and chicken stock to the pan and bring to a boil. Cook for a further 4–5 minutes, or until tender.

4 Mix the cornstarch to a paste with a little cold water and stir into the sauce to thicken. Return the chicken to the pan together with the lemon juice. Reheat and then serve immediately, garnished with fresh parsley.

Chicken Crepes

A good way of using up left-over cooked chicken and crepe batter. They make a very quick and tasty lunch or supper dish.

Serves 4

INGREDIENTS
8 oz cooked, boned chicken
2 tbsp butter
1 small onion, finely chopped
2 oz mushrooms, finely chopped
2 tbsp all-purpose flour
⅔ cup fresh or canned chicken stock
  or milk
1 tbsp fresh parsley, chopped
8 small or 4 large cooked crepes
oil, for brushing
2 tbsp grated cheese
salt and freshly ground black pepper

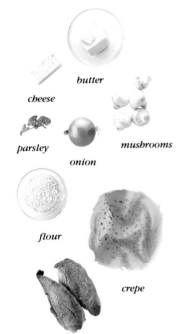

butter

cheese

parsley

mushrooms

onion

flour

crepe

chicken

1 Remove the skin from the chicken and cut into cubes.

2 Heat the butter in a saucepan and cook the onion gently until tender. Add the mushrooms. Cook with the lid on for a further 3–4 minutes.

3 Add the flour and then the stock or milk, stirring continually. Boil to thicken and simmer for 2 minutes. Season with salt and freshly ground black pepper.

4 Add the chicken and parsley.

5 Divide the filling between the crepes, roll them up and arrange in a greased ovenproof dish. Preheat the broiler.

6 Brush the crepes with a little oil and sprinkle with cheese. Broil until nicely browned. Serve hot.

Old-fashioned Chicken Pie

The chicken can be roasted and the sauce prepared a day in advance. Leave to cool completely before covering with pastry and baking. Make into four individual pies or a large one.

Serves 4

INGREDIENTS
1 × 3½ lb chicken
1 onion, quartered
1 tarragon or rosemary sprig
2 tbsp butter
4 oz button mushrooms
2 tbsp all-purpose flour
1¼ cups fresh or canned chicken
    stock
4 oz cooked ham, diced
2 tbsp chopped fresh parsley
1 × 1 lb package puff or
    flaky pastry
1 egg, beaten
salt and freshly ground black pepper

egg

flour   *butter*

button mushrooms

chicken   *onion*

ham   *pastry*

1 Preheat the oven to 400°F. Put the chicken into a casserole together with the quartered onion and the herbs. Add ½ pint water and season with salt and pepper. Cover with a lid and roast for about 1¼ hours or until tender.

4 Bring to a boil, season to taste and add the ham, chicken and parsley. Turn into one large or four individual pie dishes and cool before covering with pastry.

2 Remove the chicken and strain the liquid into a measuring cup or bowl. Cool and remove any fat that settles on the surface. Make up to ½ pint with water and reserve for the sauce.

3 Remove the chicken from the bones and cut into large cubes. Melt the butter in a pan, add the mushrooms and cook for 2–3 minutes. Sprinkle in the flour and gradually blend in the chicken stock.

5 Roll out the pastry on a lightly floured surface to 2 in larger than the pie dish. Cut a narrow strip of pastry to place around the edge of the dish. Dampen with a little water and stick to the rim of the dish. Brush the strip with beaten egg.

6 Lay the pastry loosely over the pie, taking care not to stretch it. Press firmly onto the rim. Using a sharp knife, trim away the excess pastry and knock up the sides to help encourage the pastry to rise. Crimp the edge neatly and cut a hole in the center of the pie. This allows steam to escape during cooking. Decorate with pastry leaves and chill until ready to bake.

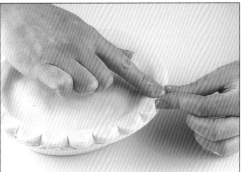

7 Brush the pastry with beaten egg (taking care not to glaze over the sides of the pastry). Bake in the preheated oven for 25–35 minutes for the small pies, and 35–45 minutes for the large one, until well risen and nicely browned all over.

COOK'S TIP

Brush the pastry with beaten egg just before baking, as the egg will begin to dry out if kept standing, and may cause cracking on the pastry.

Chicken en Croûte

Chicken breasts, layered with herbs and orange-flavored stuffing and wrapped in light puff pastry, make an impressive dish to serve at a dinner party.

Serves 8

INGREDIENTS
1 × 1 lb package puff pastry
4 large boned and skinned
  chicken breasts
1 egg, beaten

FOR THE STUFFING
4 oz trimmed leeks, thinly sliced
2 oz lean bacon, chopped
2 tbsp butter
2 cups fresh white bread crumbs
2 tbsp chopped fresh herbs,
  e.g. parsley, thyme, marjoram and
  chives
grated rind of 1 large orange
1 egg, beaten
salt and freshly ground black pepper

puff pastry

bacon

egg

leek

bread crumbs

herbs

chicken breasts

butter

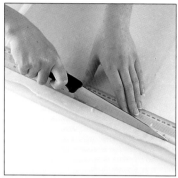

1 First make the stuffing. Cook the leeks and bacon in the butter until soft. Put the bread crumbs into a bowl with the herbs and plenty of seasoning. Add the leeks and butter with the grated orange rind and bind with the beaten egg. If the mixture is too dry and crumbly, add a little orange juice or stock to bring it to a moist consistency.

2 Roll the pastry out to a rectangle measuring 12 × 16 in. Trim the edges and reserve for the decoration.

3 Place the chicken breasts between two pieces of plastic wrap and flatten to a thickness of ¼ in with a rolling pin. Spread a third of the stuffing over the center of the pastry. Lay two chicken breasts side-by-side over the stuffing. Cover with another third of the stuffing, then repeat with more chicken breasts and the rest of the stuffing.

4 Make a cut diagonally from each corner of the pastry to the chicken. Brush the pastry with beaten egg.

5 Bring up the sides and overlap them slightly. Trim away any excess pastry before folding the ends over like a parcel. Turn over onto a greased baking sheet, so that the joins are underneath. Shape neatly and trim away any excess pastry.

6 With a sharp knife, lightly criss-cross the pastry into a diamond pattern. Brush with beaten egg and cut leaves from the trimmings to decorate the top. Bake at 400°F for 50–60 minutes or until well risen and golden brown on top.

Chicken Veronique

Small broilers are six to ten weeks old and are large enough to serve two people.

Serves 4

INGREDIENTS
2 small broilers
2 fresh tarragon or thyme sprigs
2 tbsp butter
4 tbsp white wine
grated rind and juice of ½ lemon
1 tbsp olive oil
1 tbsp all-purpose flour
⅔ cup fresh or canned chicken stock
4 oz seedless green grapes, halved
salt and freshly ground black pepper
fresh parsley, chopped, to garnish

tarragon

grapes

lemon

butter

olive oil

white wine

flour

broilers

1 Preheat the oven to 350°F. Put the herbs inside the cavity of each broiler and tie into a neat shape.

2 Heat the butter in a casserole, brown the broilers lightly all over and pour on the wine. Season with salt and pepper, cover, and cook in the oven for 20–30 minutes or until tender.

3 Remove the broilers from the casserole and cut in half with a pair of kitchen scissors, removing the backbones and small rib cage bones. Arrange on a shallow ovenproof dish. Sprinkle with lemon juice and brush with oil, then broil until lightly browned. Keep warm.

4 Mix the flour into the butter and wine in the casserole, and blend in the stock. Bring to a boil, season to taste and add the lemon rind and grapes, then simmer for 2–3 minutes. Spoon the sauce over the chickens, garnish with fresh parsley and serve immediately.

Crispy Spring Chickens

These small birds are about 2–2½ lb in weight and are delicious either hot or cold.

Serves 4

INGREDIENTS
2 × 2–2½ lb chickens
salt and freshly ground black pepper

FOR THE HONEY GLAZE
2 tbsp honey
2 tbsp sherry
1 tbsp vinegar

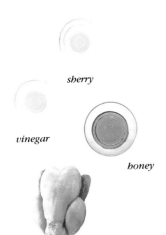

sherry

vinegar

honey

chicken

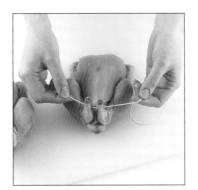

1 Preheat the oven to 350°F. Tie the birds into a neat shape and place on a wire rack over the sink. Pour over boiling water to plump the flesh and pat dry with paper towels.

2 Mix the honey, sherry and vinegar together and brush over the birds. Season with salt and pepper.

3 Place the rack into a roasting pan and bake the birds for 45–55 minutes. Baste well with the honey glaze until crisp and golden brown.

Traditional Roast Chicken

Serve with bacon rolls, chipolata sausages, gravy and
stuffing balls or bread sauce.

Serves 4

INGREDIENTS
1 × 3½ lb chicken
4 lean bacon rashers
2 tbsp butter
salt and freshly ground black pepper

FOR THE PRUNE AND NUT STUFFING
2 tbsp butter
½ cup chopped pitted prunes
½ cup chopped walnuts
1 cup fresh bread crumbs
1 egg, beaten
1 tbsp chopped fresh parsley
1 tbsp snipped fresh chives
2 tbsp sherry or port

FOR THE GRAVY
2 tbsp all-purpose flour
1¼ cups fresh or canned chicken
stock, or vegetable water

chicken

walnuts

bread crumbs

egg

chives   sherry

bacon

butter   prunes

1 Preheat the oven to 375°F. Mix all the stuffing ingredients together in a bowl and season well.

2 Stuff the neck end of the chicken quite loosely, allowing room for the bread crumbs to swell during cooking. (Any remaining stuffing can be shaped into small balls and fried to accompany the roast.)

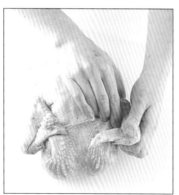

3 Tuck the neck skin under the bird to secure the stuffing and hold in place with the wing tips (pinions) or sew with thread or fine string.

4 Place in a roasting pan and cover with the bacon rashers (these help to protect the lean breast and flavor the bird as it cooks). Spread with the remaining butter, cover loosely with foil and roast for about 1½ hours. Baste with the juices in the roasting pan 3 or 4 times during cooking.

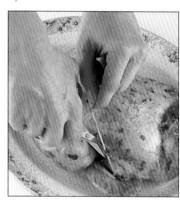

5 Remove any trussing string and transfer to a serving plate, cover with the foil and leave to stand while making the gravy. (This standing time allows the flesh to relax and makes carving easier.)

6 Carefully spoon off the fat from the juices in the roasting pan. Blend the flour into the juices and cook gently until golden brown. Add the stock or reserved vegetable water, bring to a boil, stirring until thickened. Adjust the seasoning to taste, then strain the gravy into a pitcher or gravy boat for serving.

Kotopita

This is based on a Greek chicken pie. Serve hot or cold with a typical Greek salad made from tomatoes, cucumber, onions and feta cheese.

Serves 4

INGREDIENTS
10 oz filo pastry
2 tbsp olive oil
½ cup chopped toasted almonds
2 tbsp milk

FOR THE FILLING
1 tbsp olive oil
1 medium onion, finely chopped
1 garlic clove, crushed
1 lb boned, cooked chicken
2 oz feta cheese, crumbled
2 eggs, beaten
1 tbsp chopped fresh parsley
1 tbsp chopped fresh coriander
1 tbsp chopped fresh mint
salt and freshly ground black pepper

chicken

olive oil

feta cheese

eggs

parsley

mint

almonds

onion

coriander

filo pastry

1 For the filling, heat the oil in a large frying pan and cook the onion gently until tender. Add the garlic clove and cook for a further 2 minutes. Transfer to a bowl.

2 Remove the skin from the chicken and then grind or chop it finely. Add to the onion with the rest of the filling ingredients. Mix thoroughly and season with salt and freshly ground black pepper.

3 Preheat the oven to 375°F. Have a damp dish towel ready to keep the filo pastry covered at all times. You will need to work fast, as the pastry dries out very quickly when exposed to air. Unravel the pastry and cut the whole batch into a 12 in square.

4 Taking half the sheets (cover the remainder), brush one sheet with a little olive oil, lay it on a well greased 2¼ pint ovenproof dish and sprinkle with a few chopped toasted almonds. Repeat with the other sheets, overlapping them alternately into the dish.

5 Spoon in the filling and cover the pie in the same way with the rest of the overlapping pastry.

6 Fold in the overlapping edges and mark a diamond pattern on the surface of the pie with a sharp knife. Brush with milk and sprinkle on any remaining almonds. Bake for 20–30 minutes or until golden brown on top.

INDEX